Dwarf Caiman

Julie Murray

Abdo Kids Junior
is an Imprint of Abdo Kids
abdobooks.com

Abdo
MINI ANIMALS
Kids

abdobooks.com

Published by Abdo Kids, a division of ABDO, P.O. Box 398166, Minneapolis, Minnesota 55439.
Copyright © 2020 by Abdo Consulting Group, Inc. International copyrights reserved in all countries.
No part of this book may be reproduced in any form without written permission from the publisher.
Abdo Kids Junior™ is a trademark and logo of Abdo Kids.

Printed in the United States of America, North Mankato, Minnesota.

102019
012020

THIS BOOK CONTAINS
RECYCLED MATERIALS

Photo Credits: Alamy, iStock, Minden Pictures, Shutterstock, ©NHPA/Photoshot p.21

Production Contributors: Teddy Borth, Jennie Forsberg, Grace Hansen

Design Contributors: Christina Doffing, Candice Keimig, Dorothy Toth

Library of Congress Control Number: 2019941209
Publisher's Cataloging-in-Publication Data

Names: Murray, Julie, author.

Title: Dwarf caiman / by Julie Murray

Description: Minneapolis, Minnesota : Abdo Kids, 2020 | Series: Mini animals | Includes online
    resources and index.

Identifiers: ISBN 9781532188794 (lib. bdg.) | ISBN 9781644943014 (pbk.) |
    ISBN 9781532189289 (ebook) | ISBN 9781098200268 (Read-to-Me ebook)

Subjects: LCSH: Caimans--Juvenile literature. | Reptiles--Juvenile literature. | Rain forest animals--Juvenile
    literature. | Animal size--Juvenile literature. | Size and shape--Juvenile literature.

Classification: DDC 597.984--dc23

Table of Contents

Dwarf Caiman

It is a small caiman.

It is related to alligators.

It is less than 5 feet (1.5 m) long.

It weighs 15 pounds (6.8 kg).

It lives in South America.

South America

It is found in lakes and rivers.

It also lives in ponds.

It has **scales**. They are dark in color.

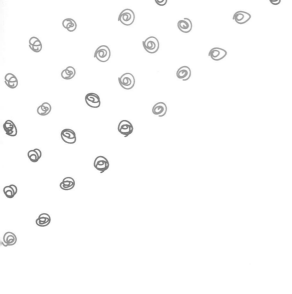

Its head is short. Its snout turns up.

It has a long tail. The tail helps it swim.

It eats fish and crabs. It also likes lizards.

Let's Compare!

dwarf caiman

American alligator

Size: 5 feet (1.5 m)
Weight: 15 pounds (6.8 kg)

Size: 13 feet (4.0 m)
Weight: 790 pounds (358 kg)

Glossary

scale
a small, thin bony plate that covers the skin of reptiles.

caiman
a reptile that is related to the alligator. Caimans live in tropical areas of North and South America.

snout
the front part of an animal's head that sticks out that includes the nose, mouth, and jaws.

Index

Abdo Kids ONLINE
FREE! ONLINE MULTIMEDIA RESOURCES

Visit abdokids.com
to access crafts, games,
videos, and more!

Use Abdo Kids code

MDK8794

or scan this QR code!